SECRET
NEWARK

Jill Campbell &
Michael Cox

AMBERLEY

This book is dedicated to the late H. Vernon Radcliffe MBE, former curator of Newark Museum, who gave us the inspiration, guidance and tutelage over many years, in local history.

Jill Campbell and Michael Cox

First published 2015

Amberley Publishing
The Hill, Stroud, Gloucestershire, GL5 4EP
www.amberley-books.com

Copyright © Jill Campbell and Michael Cox, 2015

The right of Jill Campbell and Michael Cox to be identified as the Author of this work has been asserted in accordance with the Copyrights, Designs and Patents Act 1988.

ISBN 978 1 4456 4495 0 (print)
ISBN 978 1 4456 4515 5 (ebook)

British Library Cataloguing in Publication Data.
A catalogue record for this book is available from the British Library.

Typesetting by Amberley Publishing.
Printed in Great Britain.

Contents

Introduction

This book is an attempt to set down and explain many of the little-known aspects of our market town.

Over the last thirty or so years our society (Newark Archaeological and Local History Society) has conducted guided tours for a variety of groups, both local and from abroad. During that time, much information has been accrued which may be regarded as 'secret', i.e. not generally known. Our guides never stop learning new information.

Newark owes its origin entirely to its location. The River Trent meanders its way north-eastwards through Nottinghamshire towards the River Humber where it joins the North Sea. The name 'Trent' is a descriptive title in an ancient language referring to its untamed nature.

Approaching Newark, it passes between the foothills of Derbyshire and western Nottinghamshire and the Lincolnshire lime ridge. This point at the tidal extreme has always been a crossing point on the journey down the country.

After the last ice age the cave dwellers of Derbyshire (Creswell Crags) crossed the valley on their summer migration and camped in the area of Farndon in order to gather and work the flint deposits of the river valley.

It is not known if there was a prehistoric settlement at Newark. Many of the villages located on raised ground along the valley have their origins in prehistory, but there is no evidence of such an origin for Newark.

The coming of the Romans brought changes to the area, most notably the building of the Fosse Way. This passes through the site of Newark and there are two settlements on either side, Ad Pontem at Stoke and Crococolana at Brough. If there had been a town or settlement at Newark we would expect some reference to have survived.

The first known settlement at Newark was constructed by Angles. The Roman army was almost entirely made up of peoples they had conquered. Consequently the garrisons of this country would be made up of continental, Romanised soldiers who would settle there on retirement or spread the word on returning home, that there was land to be had for settlement.

In the seventh century one such group or tribe decided that they would settle in the Trent valley and called their settlement their 'New Warke' (meaning 'new work' or 'new fortification').

This settlement is under the present site of the castle. These people were pagan originally and as a consequence an extensive cremation cemetery exists in the area of Millgate. It is one of the largest Anglo-Saxon cemeteries in the country, first discovered in the nineteenth century.

Later in the seventh century the incursions by the so-called Vikings began to occur. Newark would be vulnerable to such seaborne raiders, as the river would be navigable by their craft.

Eventually the Vikings overwintered and settled, taking over this part of the country and making it the Danelaw. This period would be unsettling for the town as it is on the border of the kingdoms of Mercia and Anglia and was probably much fought over.

The surviving vestiges of the Vikings in the town are the street names. As in other towns of the Danelaw the word 'Gate' has survived as the word for a street. Two streets in particular have their Viking name, Bargate, the street of the bar (Danish for 'street' is 'gata') and Kirkgate, the street of the kirk or church. The word 'street' has a Saxon derivation.

The country then became one under the rule of Alfred the Great's successors and Newark became part of the holdings of the monks of Stowe by Lincoln.

This was at the time when sheep farming came to the fore and the town began to prosper. The earliest wooden church would be built at this time.

In 1066 all this changed with the Norman invasion. A few years after the invasion a 'motte and bailey' castle were constructed in the area of the later stone castle and the town came under the overlordship of the Bishop of Lincoln. The Bishop, Alexander the Magnificent, wished to build a castle and because the king already had one at Lincoln, he chose the site at Newark. It was this castle that had the splendid Romanesque gate house which stands to this day. It is thought that it dates from about 1135, though timber dating in the castle's fabric gives a date of around 850. This demonstrates the re-using of oak timbers, which were a precious commodity.

Alexander also built a stone church on the site of a wooden structure and laid out most of the core of the town, as we know it today. He was also given permission to hold a market and a fair.

The town was walled but it is not clear whether this was stone or wood. Some pieces of stone remain on the known line of the wall but the rest may well have been robbed out.

In the twelfth century the Black Death struck the town and work on the church came to a standstill, as over two-thirds of the population would have died.

In later years the town settled into a prosperous period with the start of a redesigned church in the latest style and remodelling of the castle into a less defensive design by Bishop Rotherham.

Many of the town's timber-framed buildings date from this time.

The main industry of the town was wool, benefiting from the extensive flat lands on the Lincolnshire side of the town. The trade brought businessmen from Kent and the near continent to settle in the town.

The establishment of the major charities took place at this time leading to almshouses for the poor and grammar and song schools.

This prosperity continued despite the dissolution of the monasteries and closing of the chantries.

However, progress is interrupted by Civil War. Newark placed itself on the side of the King and, because of its strategic position on both the river and Great North Road, became an important location. It was besieged three times, but never fell, only submitting upon the order of the King, who surrendered to the Scots Army at Kelham in 1646.

Following the surrender the town was in a sorry state and was suffering plague and sacking.

Over the next hundred years there was a change in agriculture, with the rich fertile lands of the valley being turned over to barley. This enabled several entrepreneurs to develop brewing and malting industries in the town.

The wealth from these funded a period of rebuilding in the popular 'Georgian' style. In fact the town we see today is largely that Georgian town with a few remaining timber buildings and Victorian and twentieth-century buildings added.

The population expanded with this prosperity and increased threefold from 1800 to 1900. Toward the end of the nineteenth century, manufactories began to be set up, mainly to serve the agricultural industry in the first instance.

For the first half of the twentieth century the town could be described as an industrial town but the decline of manufacturing in the latter part of the century has left the town with a varied business base.

We hope that you will enjoy the strolls that follow and absorb more of the fascinating history of this small market town.

1. Entering Newark

Travelling into Newark along the Old Great North Road, you can understand why it deserved to be called 'Gateway to the North'. A long, straight thoroughfare leads you into the town, with its imposing castle facing you, on the banks of the River Trent.

Newark's strategic position in the country was initially determined by its being on one of the few fording places of the River Trent, along its length throughout the heart of the country, from its source on Biddulph Moor, Staffordshire, to the Humber Estuary. This is a distance of 185 miles.

Along the route, from South Muskham onwards, you may notice a series of brick 'bridges', and that the road sits higher up in the landscape. These are the remains of a raised causeway, or viaduct, designed and built by the engineer, John Smeaton in 1776, upon the instruction of Newark's Aldermen (Town Council). John Smeaton, (1724–1792) was elected a Fellow of the Royal Society in 1753. He was an English civil engineer, born in Austhorpe, Leeds, and was responsible for the design of bridges, canals, harbours and lighthouses. He was also a capable mechanical engineer and an eminent physicist. The first self-styled civil engineer, as opposed to military engineer, he was the founder of the Society of Civil Engineers in 1771. His pupils included William Jessop (1745–1814).[1]

John Smeaton (1724–1792).

Recommended by the Royal Society, Smeaton designed the third Eddystone Lighthouse (1755–59). He pioneered the use of hydraulic lime (a form of mortar that will set under water) and developed a technique involving dovetailed blocks of granite in the building of the lighthouse. His lighthouse remained in use until 1877 when the rock underlying the structure's foundations began to erode; it was dismantled and partially rebuilt at Plymouth where it is known as 'Smeaton's Tower'. He is important in the history, rediscovery and development of modern cement, because he identified the compositional requirements needed to obtain 'hydraulicity' in lime. This work led ultimately to the invention of Portland cement and to the re-emergence of concrete as a modern building material, largely due to Smeaton's influence.

This stretch of road was always prone to flooding, being low-lying, and following a particularly bad flood in the 1770s, when the villagers of Muskham were charging exorbitant sums of money to ferry travellers into the town, the viaduct was commissioned.

Listed Grade II along its length from Muskham, remains of this viaduct at the entrance to the town can be seen below the wall of the Riverside car park, opposite the old Midland Hotel (now apartments).

We face the bridge over the Trent. Built in stone in 1776, and commissioned by the Duke of Newcastle, it replaced a series of wooden structures, which naturally did not last. The increase in coach travel in the eighteenth century meant increased traffic and footfall over the bridge, so the two footpaths on either side were added in 1848. Made of cast iron, you can see the structure when walking down the little slip path towards the river, on the right hand side. A reconstructed towpath under the bridge enables you to pass across safely. Notice the flood-level mark on one of the pillars.

Smeaton's viaducts.

Trent Bridge cast-iron footpath, and towpath under bridge.

Flood-level mark under bridge.

The greatest flood that had happened in many years occurred in October 1875. Days of incessant rain led to the River Trent overflowing its banks, sending a deluge of water over the countryside. Fields were converted to lakes, dykes became huge streams and the flood rushed through the bridges in a terrifying way. The Trent Valley, as far as the eye could see, was one vast expanse of water, ruining crops and farmland. The damage caused was inestimable and not a village escaped the damage. Cattle were swept away, and the losses to householders were great. In Newark, the water was deep enough to allow four grammar schoolboys to row across the countryside to Kelham.

Returning to the other side of the road, and before we cross the bridge, notice a cut-mark on the right-hand-side pillar of the bridge facing the town. Known as 'bench-marks' these arrow-shaped cut marks were made by surveyors throughout the country during the mid-nineteenth century to determine the height above sea level of each point, to enable accurate ordnance survey map-making. These cut marks are known as 'fundamental bench marks'. There are several others throughout the town, some of which are of different types. These will be described as we come across them in our strolls.

Crossing the bridge, look at the Newark Coat of Arms on either side, bearing its motto 'Deo Fretus Erumpe' (Trust in God and Sally Forth) – a Civil War declaration, which was adopted by the town in 1912.

The official blazon reads:

Arms: Bars wavy of six Argent and Azure on a Chief Gules a Peacock in his pride proper between a Fleur-de-Lis on the Dexter and a Lion passant guardant on the sinister Or.
Crest: On a Wreath Argent and Azure a Morfex Argent beaked Sable holding in its beak an Eel proper; Mantled Gules doubled Argent.
Supporters: On the Dexter (right hand) side an Otter and on the Sinister (left hand) side a Beaver the latter 'langued gules' (the tongue visible).

The wavy bars, crest, and supporters (an otter and a beaver) refer to Newark's riverside position. The fleur-de-lis and lion are royal emblems. Local opinion describes the bird as the symbol of pride.

The granting of a crest was one of the first grants made to a civic body, the first being that made to the borough of Ipswich on 29 August 1561. Several variations of the crest have been quoted. The original grant describes the bird as a 'Morfex' holding an eel.

It raises the interesting question of what type of bird a morfex is. It is not a Latin term, nor a name for a heraldic creature; it does not feature in contemporary word-lists or vocabulary, and appears in no other grants of arms. The nearest possible equivalent is the 'morfer', included in the Oxford English Dictionary as a dialectal and obsolete word, possibly a corruption of 'morfran', the Welsh name for a cormorant.

Another possibility for the bird is the moorcock (better known as the grouse), a small bird not dissimilar to that depicted in the patent, and one that has often featured as a crest. But the bird probably was never resident in or near Newark. A more likely intention could be the moorhen, a waterfowl found to this day on the Trent, which may have been what was originally intended.

Cut benchmark.

Newark Coat of Arms.

The question of the identity of the bird featured on the crest has unsurprisingly been the subject of much debate and some error over the years. Armorists, in compiling reference works have occasionally used the Newark arms to illustrate the definition of 'morfex', usually reproducing the bird as seen on the patent. On other occasions the bird has merely been changed to a more recognisable type, such as the heraldic catch-all of the martlet. Whatever the type of bird thought to be on the crest, up until around 1900 it was invariably depicted as a seated, short-legged and short-necked creature.

In 1915 the bird was described as a cormorant, without further explanation why. Since that time the bird in question has either appeared as a golden cormorant or as a heron (or egret) in its proper colours; at any rate, it then became a long-legged and long-necked species instead of the more short-necked, short-billed species as on the original image.

The motto ('*Deo Fretus Erumpe*' – Trust in God, and Sally Forth) is a translation of the valiant words of the mayor, to Lord Bellasyse, during the siege of Newark by the Parliamentarians in 1646, at the close of the First English Civil War.[2]

The 'Ossington', presently an Italian restaurant, with apartments above, was built in 1882 by Lady Charlotte Ossington, widow of John Evelyn Dennison 1st Viscount Ossington, Speaker of the House of Commons.[3] It was built in his memory as a temperance coffee hotel. Lady Ossington was the daughter of the 4th Duke of Portland. Look upwards at the magnificent façade and the intricate details on the extra down-pipes from the roof. Down-spouts in the shape of eels! These are a passing commemoration of the fact that the River Trent was once famous for its eels.

Further along, towards the main entrance, look downward at the cast-iron drain covers set amongst the cobbles bearing the name 'J. Bazalgette'.

This famous name was most often associated with the city of London. Joseph Bazalgette (28 March 1819–15 March 1891) was a noted nineteenth-century English civil engineer. As Chief Engineer of London's Metropolitan Board of Works, his major achievement was the creation (in response to the 'Great Stink' of 1858) of a sewer network for Central London, which was responsible for relieving the city from cholera epidemics, whilst beginning the cleaning up of the River Thames.

Such was the importance of the 'Ossington Coffee Palace' at the time, and the prestigious connections of lady Ossington (who had built the Coffee Palace in memory of her late husband, Evelyn John Dennison, who was Speaker at the House of Commons).

We must now cross the Great North Road again and enter the Castle Gardens. You are now in the Parish of Stoke! Look at the unusually shaped flowerbed facing you on the right. A typical design done by the landscape gardener and civil engineer, Henry Ernest Milner (1845–1906). Milner was active on various sites both at home and abroad. Son of Edward Milner (1819–1884) he joined his father's landscape design practice in the 1870s. He wrote the definitive book *The Art & Practice of Landscape Gardening* in the 1890s. Newark Castle Gardens were laid out in 1887, to celebrate the Jubilee of Queen Victoria.[4]

Before walking down towards the riverside, glance up at the castle terrace area in front of the curtain wall. A small notice at one end informs visitors that by walking along the length of the terrace eleven times, you will have walked one mile!

Newark Castle of course, during its long history of nine hundred years, has seen many events, both local and national. The English Civil War saw Newark playing a pivotal role

Eel-shaped down-spouts on the Ossington.

Bazalgette drain covers.

Milner's flowerbeds in the castle grounds.

Terrace running along the castle's curtain wall.

in the outcome that affected the whole country. Stoutly Royalist, amid a County under mainly Parliamentarian control, it was important to King Charles for the town to keep his route to the north open, as he hoped the Scots would come to his aid. It was also important for him to aid his route to Oxford where he had set up his headquarters.

Walking along the bottom of the castle curtain wall near the riverside, and looking up at the wall, notice the circular depressions, or 'spalling', in the wall at about head height. These were caused during the English Civil War (1642–1646) by Parliamentary cannon fire from across the river. This area, known as 'The Island' during this period, was captured by Parliamentarian forces during the third and last siege of Newark in 1645/6. The cannon were of a type known as a 'Robinette', and had a calibre of about 4 cm (1.5 inches) and firing a ball weighing about 1.5 lb. Depressions higher up the wall were probably caused by larger 9-cm- (3.5-inch-) calibre cannon, firing a ball weighing about 15 lb.

We follow the riverside route along the path, to where the early Newark locks are.

Although the River Trent has been the subject of various Acts of Improvement since the seventeenth century, it has actually been used for navigation since Roman times. It has long been a vital commercial link between the Midlands and the Humber Estuary. After trans-shipment at Gainsborough or Hull, loads could go on to London or the Continent. The Romans built the Fossdyke from Torksey on the Trent to Lincoln, where it joins the River Witham. Many of the connecting rivers were made navigable in the eighteenth century: the Derwent to Derby, the Soar to Loughborough and the Idle to Bawtry.

Cannon fire 'spalling' marks from the Civil War.

Pressure to improve the Trent intensified after the opening of the Trent & Mersey Canal from Shardlow to Great Haywood in 1770, reaching the Potteries two years later. These locks were built at Newark in 1773. Further locks below Nottingham and a towpath were made in the 1780s. North of Nottingham the river was improved by making long cuts bypassing the shoals on the river itself; these works were completed by 1801. Meanwhile, the Erewash Canal had opened (1779) and the Soar Navigation improved with the construction of six locks (1780), followed by the opening of the Derby Canal (1795), Nottingham Canal (1796) and Grantham Canal (1797).

The Newark locks were extended in 1808. The weirs were installed to augment the natural depth of the river, and so provide passage for bigger barges.

We turn left at the locks, to travel up Lock Entry. Three Lock Keeper's cottages can be seen in this area, the one opposite the two points where the locks meet is the original one, and dates from 1772. The second now houses a café. The modern, latest house is on the other side of the river.

We turn right half way up the passage and walk through into Navigation Yard. The warehouse facing you was Newark Egg Packers, also warehousing, a provender mill and bagging plant. (The flourmill receives a store of wheat, eliminates all impurities from it, mills the raw material to separate flour from the bran and skin of the wheat and stores the milled products before dispatch. Provender mills provide animal feed stuffs. Historically some provender mills have formed the part of a flourmill, but today the two categories now tend to be separate). Continuing through the arch, we see in front of

Trent navigation lock – upstream.

Trent navigation lock – downstream.

Wall-tie plate – Corcoran, Witt & Co.

us a former malting building that has now been converted into housing. Note the wall plates on the building. The oval plate (which its square nut) states that it was made by a company called 'Corcoran, Witt & Co. of London'. This company were malt kiln makers, as well as makers of much of the malting equipment. The other wall plate, the round one, can be identified as being made by our own William Newsum Nicholson, of the Trent Ironworks near Trent Bridge, who were well-known and award-winning makers of much of the country's agricultural implements. This wall plate has a hexagonal nut, which was a progression from the square nut around in 1875.

Immediately beyond the passageway notice the patchwork haulage path (facing) – two tracks made from granite setts with tarmac between (the tarmac is a recent addition, the areas between the setts would originally have been rough stone). These tracks were designed to help dray horses to grip as they pulled their loads from the wharf and from the town weighbridge – the site of which can just be made out as a slightly depressed rectangular pattern in the setts. The wharf itself is now The Otter Park with an artwork, by Judith Bluck, consisting of bronze otters on top of limestone rocks.

Further along we see a five-storey building, which was originally a malting, but was extended in 1880 by the Trent Navigation Commissioners and converted into a warehouse. Next to this is a former oil-seed mill owned by James Clarke. The yard in front used to be called 'Oil Mill Yard', and once housed Millgate Social History Museum. Notice the wall plates on the building 'JC 1870', with its square nuts (overleaf).

Wall-tie plate – W. N. Nicholson.

Dray horse sets.

Wall-tie plates – James Clarke.

Row of wall-tie plates on Mill Lane.

2. Along Millgate

Our next stroll takes us down Mill Lane and into Millgate, where we return towards Newark. Once the main thoroughfare into Newark from the west, it is thought to follow the route of the Roman Fosse Way through the town. Its proximity to the river meant that much of the town's warehouses were situated along its route, and many yards leading off it housed the workers for the many trades that were plied here. The better-class houses were situated further west along the route, the prevailing wind taking the industrial smells away from the houses. A good example is The White House, near the end of Millgate, to our right, which was the home of Thomas Earp MP, 1830–1910, who was born in Derby. He came to Newark and became a partner in the firm of Gilstrap, Earp & Co., maltsters, and also Richardson, Earp & Slater, brewers. He became a town councillor and was Mayor of the Borough in 1869/70. At the 1874 General Election, he was selected as a Member of Parliament for the Borough, as a Liberal Candidate and held the seat until 1885. Earp died at the age of seventy-nine. Another prestigious house was that of Joseph Gilstrap, owner of The Hotel in Kirkgate and the father of William Gilstrap. He built what is now Millbank Nursing Home in the early 1800s.

We continue our stroll into Newark. Drawing near Parliament Street on the right hand side of Millgate, an impressive, large, double-bay brick building stands near the corner. This was the former Catholic Presbytery. It is of an early seventeenth-century build, possibly incorporating an earlier building, with late eighteenth- and early nineteenth-century alterations. Built of brick with stone dressings and hipped and gabled steep-pitched slate roofs, it is the oldest brick-built house in the town.

Moving further down Millgate we come across a small building, on the right hand side of the road, bearing a plaque which depicts this as being the first Methodist chapel in Newark. Methodism in Newark progressed from a rented room and preaching house in Northgate, to this purpose-built chapel, in 1776. The site on Northgate is not known, but a travelling preacher, Thomas Lee, recorded in his memories, 'In the winter of 1769 we met with much opposition from riotous mobs encouraged by great men. On 24 March 1770 they took the pulpit out of the preaching house and burned it in the Market Square.' It was this incident that John Eggleston, a baker, witnessed from his shop door. This resulted in his conversion and later as a steward, to invite the Revd John Wesley to open the second chapel in Barnbygate. Lee suffered much persecution during his time in Newark.

This first chapel held ten years of worship in Millgate, but as the Society increased in number, second premises had to be found.

Next door to the old chapel is a very strange and unprepossessing building. This was Newark's first Salvation Army Citadel. The Newark Corps of the Salvation Army began in the town in 1885, as an offshoot of the Southwell Corps. It was brought to the town by Mr David Henry Starr, a miller, who moved to Millgate in 1884. There had been a meeting

place opened in Cross Guns yard (in Baldertongate). Early meetings were held in the open air. On 15 June 1887 Newark Salvationists moved to their new premises in the 'Wool Hall, Millgate'. General Booth (Chief of the Salvation Army) visited on 3 August 1887, amid a great procession, flags and banners. The occasion made a collection of just over £100 towards the new hall.

We next walk to the end of Millgate, and begin our next stroll.

Opposite above: Former Catholic Presbytery, the oldest brick building in Newark.

Opposite below: Newark's first Methodist Chapel.

Above: Newark's first Salvation Army Citadel.

3. Along Castlegate and Through into the Market Place

Standing at the top of Millgate at the exit from Lock Entry we see to our left the rise to the level of Castlegate. This is the corner of the medieval walled town, and is called Castle Rising.

The width of the road at this point is probably due to the space required in front of the castle wall for defensive purposes that would also be used as a space for markets and fairs before, or in addition to, the current market square.

Walking along towards the castle we pass on our left restored Georgian cottages of a typical design for the town and constructed from the locally quarried clay bricks.

These cottages still retain wooden rectangular-section guttering that would have preceded cast iron for this purpose. The next properties after a gap are two of the town's fourteenth-century timber-framed buildings. Note the jettying of the first floor, a feature that occurred very early on in Newark probably due to its good communications with London.

There is a small building across the street with an unusual chimney. This is also timber framed, indicating the width of the street even in those early days.

The next range of Georgian buildings contains the entrance to the Swan & Salmon yard, the location of one of Newark's earliest recorded pubs built to serve the river trade.

Continuing, on our left, is Newark's earliest post office. Examination of the brickwork reveals the hinges for the original doors and higher up on the first floor are two ceramic insulators which would bring in the electricity from one of the private generator companies that operated in the days before the electricity supply was nationalised. Newark, sited as it is at the junction of the Great North Road and the Fosse, must have been of considerable importance during the early years of the Post Office. It has been established that one existed in the town as early as 1661. The first post office in Newark operated from the Saracens' Head, a coaching inn in the Market Place. In 1798, Mrs Guthrie was named as Postmistress in the building adjoining the Corn Exchange, which was built on the site of a mansion owned by Mr Guthrie, her husband. The post office continued here until about 1856, when it was moved to the end of Wilson Street.

The next building on the left is the Corn Exchange, built in 1847 by Henry Duesbury of Derby. It has always had alternative uses – as an assembly room, tea dances, boxing matches, roller-skating, bingo and a nightclub have all been held there.

The Georgian brick building, one along, has unusual brickwork. Designed to show off the owner's wealth, notice the bond of the bricks, a particular bond known as Flemish. The bond is highlighted by having the stretchers (the longer side) and headers (the end) in different colours, the stretchers being darker than the end bricks. This is achieved in the firing where the longer and hotter the firing, the darker the brick. This is more costly and therefore is an indication of wealth.

Wooden guttering.

Newark's first post office.

The next entrance on the left is the access to Cuckstool Wharf where scolds (normally women!) were ducked for their pains and, no doubt the ancient testing for witchcraft was carried out. If you drowned you were innocent, if you survived, i.e. the water rejected you, you were found guilty and put to death by some other foul means.

We must now walk along to the Registration Office, which was the former Gilstrap Free Library. Sir William Gilstrap (1816–1896), was the second son of Joseph Gilstrap, and was born in his father's Inn The Hotel, on Kirkgate. He took over his father's malting business on North Gate, Newark and (through exploiting the burgeoning rail network), turned it into a business of national importance.

In 1855 he bought the prestigious Winthorpe House in the village of Winthorpe, moving seven years later to a large hunting estate at Fornham Park near Bury St Edmunds in Suffolk.

In July 1883, the Gilstrap Free Library, his gift to the town of his birth, was opened in Newark, being the first free public library in the town. Today, the building on Castle Gate, although no longer a library, continues to serve the public.

William's coat of arms (Gilstrap) bears the crest of a hand bearing a calthrop. The name 'Gilstrap' is a derivation of this word. This is a metal device with four projecting spikes, so arranged that when three of the spikes are on the ground, the fourth points upward, used as a hazard to pneumatic tyres or to the hooves of horses. The Gilstrap coat of arms crest, which is shown on the tops of the two lamps either side of the gate, is described as 'a cubit arm erect in armour proper grasping an escutcheon gules charged with a galtrap argent'.

Next, we cross the road turning right on reaching the other side.

Walking along the pavement in front of the row of fine Georgian houses, now mostly restaurants, we find on our left an archway. This is one of the town's yards, called the Coach & Horses yard, after a public house that once stood about half way down the yard, where the bend now is. Along the wall on our right as we enter is an unusual sloping stone ledge. The usual explanation for this is that it was installed by the house owner on Castlegate to prevent the alley being used as a urinal by customers from the pub! It is apparent that any one (gentleman) relieving himself against this wall would find that the liquid would be redirected onto his shoes!

Moving further along and round an S bend, the site of the original inn, we emerge into Middlegate.

Across from the yard we are faced with the frontage of Newark's covered market, a fine cast-iron and glass structure erected by the corporation in 1884. The street façade has an early version of the town crest with the motto 'Our Chartered Rights'. This is a reference to the tensions between the Duke of Newcastle, the land owner, who was able to control the open-air market, and the corporation (first incorporated by Royal Charter in 1549), who wanted to have a market of their own.

The building was modified in the late 1980s with a mezzanine floor to provide extra space. Older townsfolk remember fondly the lockup stalls that originally filled this space. The new development, whilst being visually attractive, has been slow to achieve commercial success. Also it is named the Buttermarket, which is not strictly correct. Note the cut benchmark on the right-hand side of the brickwork.

It is worth climbing the stairs to view the fine cast-iron work supporting the roof.

Gilstrap's Coat of Arms.

Calthrop embellishment.

Coach & Horses yard.

Coat of Arms – 'Our Chartered Rights'.

Continuing through the stone arched doors we enter the Buttermarket proper. The stone floor and stone pillars were designed to keep the produce sold here cool. Designed by John Carr of York, the Town Hall and Assembly rooms above are a fine example of his work. On the left can be seen the cells of the town's Borough Police Station which was in the left-hand wing of the Town Hall. Newark Borough Police Force was established in 1835. Two forces were initially formed – a night force and a day force, each with two constables. This was later increased to six. Each was under the control of a separate superintendent. The uniform included a single-breasted blue suit with white buttons marked with the Crown and the word 'Police'. The collar was worn over a high leather stock and fastened with a brass buckle. An embroidered loop indicated the letter and number of the officer. Trousers were known as 'pegtops', boots were half Wellingtons and every officer wore a tall chimney top hat with leather top and leather supports on either side. Complete with truncheon and rattle the uniform was extremely heavy – and members of the force had to wear it constantly. It wasn't until 1869 that officers were allowed to wear their own clothes when off duty.

Alongside strict instructions to guard against gossiping and fraternising with the public are the following precise rules on the use of the police whistle: 'One sharp blast is to attract the attention of a colleague; two rather long blasts are intended to convey the intimation that you require assistance; three long blasts notify that you are in distress and danger, and that you require help at once!'

The County police wore a different-style uniform. The County police building was in Appletongate, built in 1870.

After the Second World War the Newark Borough Force amalgamated with the Nottinghamshire Constabulary. Newark's last Chief Constable Reginald Millhouse chose to continue serving as a superintendent in the new force. It was in this year that a separate traffic and communications division was established.

The Town Hall contains a grand assembly room and a small but well-presented museum and art gallery devoted to the Town's civic history and a wealth of work by local artists. Built by John Carr of York in 1773, it replaced the 'Moot Hall' (or 'King's Hall') on the north side of the Market Place, now a Starbucks coffee shop.

Continuing ahead we emerge into the market square. To our left, over the arched doorway of the Town Hall wing, notice a small holed drilled centrally into the coping stone. This once held the blue lamp, which shone over the door into the Borough Police Station. For decades during and after the Borough Police existed in the Town Hall, mothers would warn their children that, unless they behaved they would take them 'up them Town Hall steps'! Notice too, another benchmark (known as a 1GL Bolt) cut into the stonework, near the base. A different form of ordnance mark (a Flush Bracket No. BM0637) is on the base of the opposite wing.

To our left, and tucked away in a corner of the market place is a pubic house, called Sir John Arderne. This building, previously housing a millinery business, was opened in 1828 by Lord Middleton (Henry Willoughby from Wollaton Hall, Nottingham) as a subscription library called the Newark Stock Library. The upper floor was taken over as a Newsroom, which became a sort of a 'Gentleman's Club'. For fifty years it continued to grow and show a modest profit. However, with the arrival of William Gilstrap's Free

Right: Cut benchmark.

Below: Buttermarket.

Prison cells.

Site of blue lamp.

1GL bolt benchmark.

Flush bracket benchmark.

Sir John Arderne public house.

Library, by the late 1880s its demise was inevitable. After a slow decline, it finally closed in 1923.

John Arderne was born around 1307, and was one of the first English surgeons of his time who actually achieved workable treatments. His remedies for illness are considered substantial for his time, recommending opium as a soporific and as an external anaesthetic for surgery. He developed several treatments, notably for a painful affliction suffered by knights, who from long periods spent on horseback, developed painful abscesses and piles. He also developed an ointment for arrow wounds, and an enema made out of hemlock, opium and henbane in 1376.

In his early life he lived in Newark, but was in London by 1370, where he was admitted as a member to the Guild of Surgeons. He saw service in the Hundred Year's War and served in the army of the Duke of Lancaster. The injuries he saw there informed his medical writings for many years. Near the end of a long life, he was made Master Surgeon.

As we stand and look around at the Market Place, we see an area that retains its mediaeval layout. The eighteenth and nineteenth centuries see the increase in its importance as a market centre, and assuming many of the features of a modern town centre.

On the north side, we see a colonnaded building (now Starbucks). This started life as the forerunner to the Town Hall, the 'Moot Hall' (or meeting place), where the courts of the important Manor of Newark were held. The coat of arms on its front was placed there in 1708, and is that of John Holles, Duke of Newcastle, charged with that of his wife, Margaret Cavendish. This building was heavily restored in 1968, but dates from the early eighteenth century, the third one that existed on this site.

View of Newark Market Place.

On our right, and sandwiched between the Town Hall and the bank on the corner of Stodman Street, sits a narrow house, nicknamed 'The smallest house in Newark'. Now part of the Town Hall complex, it actually may well predate the Town Hall by fifty years or so. When the original bank was built on the corner of Stodman Street and the Market Place, a portion of the house was taken within their building and the rest was incorporated in the south wing of the Town Hall, probably to have been used by the Mayor's Officers. When Princess Anne opened Southfield House in the early 1970s, she came into the Town Hall to collect the purses for the Save the Children charity. It was decided to put in a toilet for her convenience in the smallest house, adjacent to the Mayor's Parlour; today the 'Sitting Room' is the Mayor's Robing Room, and the 'bedroom' up the steep narrow and twisting stairs, is a room now used by the caretaking team.

On the wall of the bank, next door, notice the Royal Doulton ceramic plaque, telling the story of Alderman Hercules Clay, and his deliverance from death in the Civil War. This plaque, probably erected when the bank was built early in the twentieth century, is one of several Doulton plaques in the town that commemorate various buildings of historic note.

Many of the principal town businesses and buildings were becoming concentrated in the Market Place and the streets leading out of it. Being on the Great North Road, Newark was an important stopover for travellers between London and Edinburgh. Three coaching inns were situated along the south side – the White Hart, the Saracen's Head and the Clinton Arms, with yards stretching back to Lombard Street, which was the route along which traffic entered Newark along the Great North Road. The Clinton had stabling for over fifty horses and eighteen bedrooms. The Saracen's Head had stabling for over forty

Smallest house in Newark.

Mayor's Robing Room.

Staircase.

horses, extensive carriage houses and livery stabling. Note the prestigious brickwork on the front of the Clinton Arms. The front is built completely with header bricks. This is not only of a more complicated design, but also would use more bricks. It is one of only two buildings in the town done in this way (the other being Northgate House).

The Clinton also has a claim to fame, in that from one of its windows a twenty-three-year-old man, in 1832, gave his first Parliamentary speech as a Tory MP candidate for Newark for the Party. He was Newark's MP from December 1832 to 1849.

William Ewart Gladstone was later elected Prime Minister of Britain and Ireland four times between 1868 and 1894. Two of the legacies of his time in Nottinghamshire are the restoration of Nottingham Castle and development of the Park Estate.

Gladstone resigned his seat in Newark in 1846 and went on to become a founder of the Liberal party. Educated at Eton College and Christ Church, University of Oxford, Gladstone had considered a life in the church but his father persuaded him to go into politics.

The name of the former Newark MP lives on in the form of the Gladstone bag, a precursor to the suitcase, named after him by a London designer.

The Duke of Newcastle had been looking for a candidate for his Newark constituency. Newark was a 'nomination borough', (or commonly called a 'rotten borough'. These were one of the curiosities of the British electoral system. Rotten boroughs were a product of a system that did not want change, where fathers passed on constituencies (and the power of MPs that went with them) to their sons as if they were personal property. In many such boroughs the very few electors could not vote for whom they truly wanted

Clinton Arms.

due to the lack of a secret ballot or simply due to the lack of a candidate in line with their political philosophy. The term 'rotten borough' came into use in the eighteenth century, and was used to mean a parliamentary borough with a tiny electorate, so small that voters were susceptible to control in a variety of ways. The word rotten had the connotation of corruption as well as that of long-term decline. Newark had been spared in the 1832 Reform Act. Sir John Gladstone was a friend of the Duke' and suggested his son would make a good MP. That son was William Ewart Gladstone.

The White Hart, on the corner of the Market Place, has a fifteenth-century ornate frontage, called pargetting, and painted in original colours. This form of decoration was more commonly found on the Continent. The plaster figures arranged along the front depict St Barbara (an early Christian martyr) who is one of the Patron Saints of brewers, and St Anthony of Padua, with his book of sermons; he is one of the Patron Saints of travellers. The range of buildings running back from this frontage are considerably older, and date from the early fourteenth century. Originally the White Hart would have opened out into Cartergate.

Although inns had existed on the sites of both the Clinton and the Saracen's Head in medieval times, these two buildings date from about 1710. They follow the popular style of the time, that of the classical Palladian pattern. It was a time when people of note were travelling to the Continent to visit the ancient Roman and Greek cities, wanting to emulate their buildings back home. The pillars that front both sides of the Market Place were an attempt to copy an Italian piazza. The pavements bordering the area were the first to be paved in the town.

Opposite these coaching inns, and on the corner of Bridge Street, stands the provision shop of Porter's. This formerly housed the printing business of Samuel and John Ridge. This prestigious printing firm, from early in the nineteenth century, was responsible for several important publications in the town at that time. The most famous of which was the poet, Lord Byron, whose ancestral home lay nearby at Newstead Abbey. The first volume of his poems was printed here in 1806. Entitled *Fugitive Pieces*, it caused an outcry when published, for its 'naughty poems' and 'too voluptuous styling' – too unsuitable, at the time, for the eyes of ladies. Byron immediately recalled as many of the books as possible and burned them. However, one complete copy still remains. Sixty-two years later, with Byron's reputation firmly established, a facsimile reprint of the original work in 1886 (itself a rare item) can be seen in Newark Library. Notice the Doulton plaque.

The first newspaper to be published in Newark appeared in 1791 – called *The Newark Herald*. It was printed by Daniel Holt at his premises in Stodman Street (now the Costa Coffee shop at the corner of St Mark's Lane). This only lasted for 156 issues, as in 1793, Daniel Holt was successfully prosecuted by the government for seditious libel. After publishing two radical political tracts on parliamentary reform (Thomas Paine's 'The Rights of Man'), he was fined £50 and condemned to two years' imprisonment.

Ridge's premises.

4. Exterior of St Mary Magdalene Church

At the south door walk west towards the tower end of the church. During Henry VIII's English Reformation Roman Catholic images within churches were defaced or destroyed. If we look up to the base of the tower you will see that the statues have been removed from the lower niches of the tower but those higher up remain; presumably there were limits to the enthusiasm of those who saw them as idolatrous.

Rounding the corner to stand under the west door we get a good impression of the splendid tower and steeple, one of the highest in the country on a parish church at 80 metres, and proving that wealth from the wool trade rather than simple accommodation for worship was the driving force behind a magnificent building such as this. They built it because they could.

The two ends of the side aisles at this end of the church are later additions to the main fabric and from their styles it is obvious that they were added at different times. Originally the base of the tower would have been on the west wall of the nave.

Looking into the centre of the road in front of the west door is a plaque, placed to commemorate all the 'Newarks of the World'. There is one in Natal (South Africa) and one in Queensland (Australia) otherwise all are in the USA. Some such as Newark in New Jersey (USA) are actually named after this town, but others are towns founded by Jewish communities and originally called the 'New Ark'.

Moving around the northwest corner and into North Church Walk we see on our left the Magnus Song School,[1] the third such building on the site, and specifically built with a room that is a perfect cube in order that the boys can rehearse in a good acoustic space. This can be seen from the outside from the height of the first-floor string course, which is higher on the southeast corner than at the north side of the building.

Also on our left, at ground level over the wall, we see a row of slate gravestones laid flat. On the bottom portion of some stones can be seen alphabets carved by stonemasons or their apprentices as practice. This section of the stone would be in the ground when the stone was upright.

The area to our left was originally called Parson's Mount and the vicarage stood there. The vicarage then moved to the fine Queen Anne house in Appletongate (now a children's nursery). The current vicarage is a modern house in the grounds of the Queen Anne house.

The original vicarage was demolished in at the beginning of the nineteenth century when the bricks etc. were sold to the head master of the Magnus Grammar School, Revd John Burdett Wittenoom, who constructed the Georgian extension to his school that faces the eastern end of church walk. This enabled him to enrol more pupils that could board (and thus accrue more revenue) and give him living accommodation.

In the centre of the churchyard is a stone slab commemorating the remains of the Civil War officers formerly buried in the church crypt, and buried in the churchyard in 1883.

Niches in church tower.

'Newarks of the World' plaque.

Magnus Song School.

Slate gravestones.

Among the gravestones around the walls are two cast-iron examples by a local iron founder. Commemorating the resting place of William Brydges (who died in 1835 aged fifty-eight) and his family. He was the Newark parish church organist for thirty-two years.

Somewhere in this north churchyard is a most unusual gravestone. Sadly the passage of time and the growth of moss have made it difficult to locate. It reads 'In memory of Uh Wus Sig Gee Gigh Goo Quay, wife of Waungudans of the Phippeway Indians of North America, who died 25 November 1847 aged forty-five years'. It is not known who she was and why she died in Newark.

On the right is a small door, which gave access to the vicar from the original location of the vicarage.

If we walk across the graveyard/park to the corner of Mount Lane, there is a small, hedged area that contains the grave of Edward Marshall, who died in 1844 aged eighty-two years, and who was a soldier whose entire history is carved on the stone. In 1778 he enlisted in the 3rd Regiment of Foot and served during the American War of Independence.

Walking a little further down Mount Lane, on your right above a garage door is a plaque with instructions where to stand and look to see the hole in the church spire caused by a cannon ball in the English Civil War. This can clearly be seen at the bottom left of the central window. Daylight is visible as the hole lines up with the window on the opposite side of the spire. During restoration of the church spire, cannon balls were found in the

Cast-iron gravestones.

Above: View of north churchyard.

Left: Grave of Edward Marshall.

Hole in the church spire.

stonework, and a near-contemporary report confirms its validity. The following entry in the churchwarden's accounts from 1644, reads: 'To Thomas Maples for three Daies work about ye First and Third Bell – Ten shillings for Bread and Beare for Souldiers for taking them up – Twelve pence'.

The mayor was passing the church when rather discordant sounds from the bells and crashing thuds were heard. On investigation, he found the four soldiers and churchwardens trying to haul the repaired bells from the floor of the church back into the belfry above. It was quite evident that the rather liberal intake of strong beer was having an effect on their judgement in completing their task. The bells kept crashing against the stone walls of the tower. A few years later, judgement was made at York for a strict limit to be applied to contracts for repair work in churches, and also the amount of beer to be consumed!

Standing on the corner of Mount Lane looking towards the church there is a good view of the length of the nave and chancel. Above the junction of the nave and chancel is a small housing for a bell. This is the Sanctus bell (so called because it is rung during the Sanctus at the Eucharist). The Sanctus bell is rung during the liturgy to call attention to an important moment.

Retrace your steps to Church Walk and turn left.

Walking towards Appletongate it will be noticed that the path is downhill. This is because we have crossed the line of the medieval town wall and its rampart.

Turn right into Appletongate and walk across to the South Church Walk. Now walk up the hill to the top of the town rampart again. The gas lamp standards were the first gaslights in the town (1832) and on installation caused disturbances as the 'ladies of the night' used this as a popular corner for their activities!

The lamps lasted long after the advent of electricity and became the last active gas lamps in the town. They were eventually converted due to a lack of spare parts and that the illumination they offered was insufficient for a modern town.

The next landmark on this walk is the large brick chimney on your left. This is the chimney for the church heating system installed in the restoration of Gilbert Scott. This chimney served a boiler originally located under the vestry. Heat was circulated under the floorboards of the church, making a huge difference to the comfort of the congregation. A gas boiler replaced the coal boiler; the chimney is no longer used but remains an interesting feature of the town. A plaque commemorates this feature.

The south door concludes the external tour of the church.

Above: Sanctus bell-tower.

Opposite above: Site of town rampart.

Opposite below: Town rampart.

Church heating chimney.

5. Interior of St Mary Magdalene Church

The Parish Church of St Mary Magdalene, one of the finest and largest parish churches in the country, was the third church on this site. Of the Saxon church built in the Manor of Earl Leofric and his wife, Lady Godiva, nothing remains. They gave Newark as an endowment to the monks of Stow, near Lincoln. A new church was built around 1180 by the Bishop of Lincoln and given to the Gilbertine priory of St Katherine in Lincoln. Little remains of this earlier church, only the four large piers at the crossing (where the transept meets the nave) and the crypt.

The present western tower was begun in 1230 and the church began to take on cathedral-like proportions. In 1227 Henry III gave six oaks from Sherwood Forest for repairs to the church. The next two hundred years saw a rebuild of the entire church, except for the tower. The south aisle was completed as were the upper stages of the tower and spire before the coming of the Black Death in the middle of the fourteenth century. About this time the area to the east of the church (bordering on Appletongate) was enclosed to enable the burial of plaque victims. The rest of the church saw sporadic building due to the reduced population. It is said that a third of the entire population died during this time. Building was not completed until the beginning of the fifteenth century.

We enter the church by the south door, and begin our stroll of the interior of this magnificent building. Within the porch on the left-hand side is a stone staircase by George Gilbert Scott, leading up to the Bishop White library (accessible by appointment only). Bishop Thomas White, in his will of 1698, left all his printed books 'to be a library, at least the good beginnings of a library, to the Mayor, Aldermen and Vicar of the towne of Newark upon Trent for the use of them and the inhabitants of that towne and the gentlemen and clergy of the adjacent countrey'. Bishop White had been Vicar of Newark from 1660 to 1666. He finally became Bishop of Peterborough in 1685. Owing to his refusal to take the oath of allegiance to William and Mary in 1689, he was deprived of his see in 1690, and spent the rest of his life in retirement.

His will further ordered that the library should be constructed within a month and the books carried there 'at the upper end of the church ... and make a room there to separate the place where they stand from other parts of the church, with a lock and key'. The vicar was charged with the security of the library and checked each year.

Although this staircase was designed during the 1855 restoration of the church, funds for its construction were not available until 1860. Until this time, access to the library was by means of a ladder.

Entering the church proper, turn left and proceed to the baptistery. On the left is the Markham monument moved here from Cotham church. It depicts Anne, daughter of John Warburton of Cheshire, Knight, and who was wife of Robert Markham of Cotham, Esquire. She died in 1711. The monument also shows her four daughters and three sons.

Stairs to Bishop White's Library.

The font itself is in two parts. The supporting pillar is fifteenth century but the bowl was destroyed during the English Civil War and replaced by the present bowl in 1660. Scott moved the font to its present position during the Great Restoration of the 1850s. It was originally situated west of the cross aisle between the North and South porches. Originally the font would have had a pinnacle cover, but this was lost during a later restoration.

Continuing to the right across the nave we must pause and look eastward and notice that the choir is set at an obtuse angle to the nave. This is not a careless building technique, but a representation of Christ's head on the cross. Called a 'weeping chancel'.

Walk across to the café area. The pillar on your right has a masonic memorial with all the symbols of the order. To the left, at the west end of the north aisle is a stone carving depicting the Holy Trinity, a three-headed figure representing God as three people. The Trinity Guild, granted in Newark between 1216 and 1272 by Henry III, held great power and influence in Newark. At this time, and up until 1549 when the first Borough Charter was granted, it represented the Town Council, controlling its affairs. Following the granting of the first charter the Guild's officers became the town's first aldermen.

The Guild Chapel was in the South Transept and it is here that the curious Trinity Stones would have been seen originally. These sorts of carvings were customary in churches.

Markham monument.

Font.

Holy Trinity stone.

A writer of 1579 reported, 'they in their churches and masse books doe paint the Trinitie with three heads or faces on one neck'. The Guild was dissolved in 1547, along with other Newark Guilds and Chantries, and all their properties in the town confiscated during the English Reformation of Henry VIII.

Guilds formed a very important part of town life. They were the welfare state and social services of their day, providing both financial and physical care, as well as spiritual support. Other Guilds in the town, representing both merchant and trade, provided care and even a pension to their members in need.

Walking eastward past the north door we see the large painting *The Raising of Lazarus* by the artist William Hilton RA. Hilton was born in Lincoln in 1786 and died in London in 1839. He was said to be one of the most eminent artists in the country at this time, and was for many years Keeper of the Royal Academy. This painting (said to be his finest work) was hung over the high altar prior to the restoration by Scott.

Moving eastwards we come to the north transept and a work *Crucifixion* by the local artist Robert Kiddey. The transept is used for exhibitions and Sunday school.

The north chancel aisle contains many interesting memorials, the most notable of which is the memorial brass to Alan Flemyng and his wife Alice, which is the largest Flemish brass in the country. Alan was a wool merchant in the town during the fourteenth century. The Flemyngs also founded a chantry, one of at least eighteen associated with the church. This is remarkable as Nottingham (then a similar-sized town) had only one.

Chantries were foundations where a chantry priest would be employed in perpetuity to sing a mass daily for the soul of the donor and his family. Newark's 'Chauntry' was the

Above: Raising of Lazarus painting by William Hilton RA (1786–1839).

Left: Memorial Brass of Alan Flemyng.

residence of these priests. Chantries were dissolved along with the monasteries in the reigns of Henry VIII and his son Edward VI.

The Merying chantry chapel is on the right of the Flemyng brass.

In front of us is the St George's Chapel, which serves as the memorial to the town's regiments and contains a memorial to the former pupils of the Magnus Grammar School who fell in the two world wars.

Moving across to the south aisle we pass the entry to the treasury. This is in the crypt of the earlier transitional-style church and once contained the coffins of the Royalist officers killed during the English Civil War sieges of Newark.

These burials have been removed to a plot in the burial ground on the north side of the church. The brass coffin plates of previous burials in the crypt are fixed to the wall to left and right at the foot of the stairs. The treasury now contains a collection of silver from village churches around the town and the silver donated by Lady Leeke to replace that disposed of, or that struck into siege coins during the Civil War. The oldest piece is the chalice said to have been used by Charles I during his visits to the town.

Emerging from the crypt we are facing the large east window by Hardman. Installed in memory of Prince Albert, consort to Queen Victoria. The south aisle east window is made up of the surviving pieces of mediaeval stained glass that survived the iconoclasm of the Commonwealth under Oliver Cromwell. Notice the more intense colour when compared with the central window.

Coffin plates in crypt.

Moving into the south aisle and walking west again, we can see on our left the Markham chantry chapel provided in a will by Robert Markham in 1505. This and that of Thomas Meyring (1500) on the other side of the High Altar, were built over the tombs of the donors. Thomas Meyring left 'all my clipped wole and all my floke of shepe' to pay for it. Here chantry priests would say daily masses for the repose of their souls. On the side of the Markham chapel is a remarkable survivor of the medieval church decoration in the form of a 'dance of death'.

High on the wall to our right is the memorial to Hercules Clay who has a remarkable story and is also commemorated by a plaque on the site of his house in the Market Place (on the NatWest Bank).[1]

Moving on to our left are some of the earliest 'Poppy head' pew ends, installed around 1525, and to our right past the entrance to the vestry is the organ case. The church, thanks to the Magnus, together with the Brown and Philipott charities, has always valued its music and so only the best instrument was installed. In 1804 funds were provided for a new organ by George Pike, the country's foremost organ builder of the time. In 1836 the organ was moved to the rood screen. As part of the major restoration of the church interior by Sir George Gilbert Scott, the organ was again relocated to its present position; Scott designed the central part of the current case. With the appointment of Samuel Reay as Master of the Song School, 'Father' Willis, the founder of a famous firm of organ builders, was engaged to rebuild the organ. This organ has been restored several times with the addition of a remote console, but remains a fine instrument.

Silver chalice used by Charles I.

Right: 'Dance of Death' plaque.

Below: Memorial to Hercules Clay.

Parish Church organ.

Move on to the crossing and return to the south door. Turn toward the centre of the church and at the nave crossing turn to face the altar. Moving up the central nave aisle, on the right are the civic pews for the mayor and town councillors. Note also the twin brackets for the town's two maces to hang during the service.

On the floor in front of us is a plaque marking the resting place of the coffin containing the remains of General Sikorski. Prime Minister of Poland during the Second World War, General Sikorski was killed in an air crash in Gibraltar and was buried in the town's Polish cemetery. His wish was that his remains should be returned to his native country only when it was free. When the USSR was disbanded, and Poland became independent, his remains were returned. A mass was celebrated in church in the presence of Prince Philip, Duke of Edinburgh. This would be the first Roman Catholic mass to be celebrated in the church since the Reformation.

Moving forward through the rood screen we are in the choir. The rear pews have a collection of medieval misericords, dating from the early sixteenth century. These are special folding seats for the lay clerks to rest whilst appearing to stand up and are traditionally carved on the underside with rustic scenes.

In front of us is the high altar. If you are not here in Lent, you will see the full spread of the Ninian Comper reredos (a decorative facing as the wall behind the altar). This 1920s piece was installed over the top of the reredos installed by Gilbert Scott. During Lent the Comper reredos is folded in on itself, allowing visitors to glimpse the Scott reredos that

Plaque to General Sikorski.

Misericords.

Above: Reredos ordered by Sir George Gilbert Scott.

Opposite: Memorial to Robert Ramsey, 1639.

appears to be in the style of the Pre-Raphaelite Brotherhood. The two reredos have always courted controversy, some preferring the Scott design and others the rather Byzantine splendour of that by Ninian Comper.

At the rear of the choir are three painted plaster memorials to town dignitaries. Robert Ramsey (died 1639) on the north-west corner of the chancel, he is depicted wearing a slashed doublet with a large square-cut white collar. He has a small moustache and a pointed beard. According to his epitaph, he was killed by lightning. On the south side of the chancel is Thomas Atkinson, who was mayor in 1641. He is depicted in a close-fitting doublet with puff sleeves and white ruff. He wears a long moustache and small beard. During the Civil War, he was the leader of the inhabitants of Newark. He was mayor in 1641. In the south-west corner of the north choir aisle is the plaster monument is to John Johnson. He is depicted wearing a gown and a large ruff. He has a small moustache and beard. A staunch Royalist, he was mayor in 1639 and four times deputy mayor. He established a charity for poor widows and also for the maintenance of the church windows. As an alderman, he took charge of the Magnus rental monies and supported the grammar school.

Now make your way to the south door and exit into the South Church Walk.

HEERE LYETH Ye BODY OF ROBART RAMSEY, SERVANT
TO HIS MAties WHO DYED Ye 9 DAY of APRILL 1639

THIS DVST IS HIS, WHO PAST HIS YEARES
AS VOYD OF CRYMES, AS NOW OF FEARES
TRVE TO HIS GOD, AND TO HIS FREIND
HIMSELFE IN NEITHER, HIS OWNE END
ONE OF A CHASTE, AND CONSTANT LIFE
AN HVSBAND ONLY, TO HIS WIFE
HIS ACTIONS SVCH, AS IF THAT HEE
LIVD NOT TO Th TYME BVT MEMORY
ALL MANAGD STILL, WITH THAT INTENT
TO MAKE HIS NAME, HIS MONVMENT
RIDINGE SECVRE, GOD ON THE WAY
SPAKE FROM A CLOVD, & BID HIM STAY
HIS VERTVES KEPT, THAT EQVALL GVARD
HEE COVLD NOT BE, CALLD VNPREPARD
SOE WELL COMPOSD, STILL SO ADVISD
THAT HE, THOVGH SEIZD, WAS NOT SVRPRIZED
THVS GOD MEN ARE, BY NOE CHANGE HARMD
READY TO YEILD, BVT ALLWAIES ARMD

Memorial to Thomas Atkinson, 1661.

Memorial to John Johnson, 1659.

6. Stodman Street, Middlegate and Kirkgate

Standing on Castlegate looking up Stodman Street, formerly Stodmere Street, suggesting a pool or pond in the locality, we see a mixture of old and new buildings. The first building of interest is The Prince Rupert public house. This was formerly the Woolpack, a name that more accurately links with its past.

The house was possibly the home of a wool merchant who had moved from the Kentish wool industry to ply his trade in Newark. On moving, he would set-up home in a suitable house. His idea of a suitable house would be what he was used to at home in Kent. Therefore in the Midlands we have an example of a Kentish yeoman's or Wealden house. Consisting of a central hall, the full height of the building, with a two-storey section at each end, jettied over the street.

The house as we now see it is only half of the original but investigations of the roof timbers show that it was once a complete Wealden building of twice the street frontage. A fifteenth-century house, it has recently been sympathetically restored.

Further along on the same side of the road is the former Harston's music shop. This shop front has interesting Doric pilasters at each side of the window and an ornamental facia; these may reflect an earlier usage.

We then reach the junction with Middlegate and turn left. The shop immediately on our left is a former ironmonger's shop; the archway to the rear of the premises can still be made out.

The next building has a 'v' section window at first- and second-floor level. This was the former Savoy cinema. Built in 1935 in the Art Deco style complete with café and ballroom, it was closed in the 1970s after an unsuccessful conversion to multiscreen.

A little further along we come to the crossing of two streets, Chain Lane and Boar lane. Over the years due to rebuilding the two streets no longer quite line up but these streets in fact represent the original route of the Great North Road through the town.

The building on the corner of Chain Lane was an inn, The Duke of Cumberland, with a coaching entrance onto Middlegate. Next to this building and before the arrival of the covered Market Hall, was the site of the first Newark Theatre.

This end of Boar Lane is lined with early Georgian brick buildings. On the right a little ahead in Middlegate is a large town house in the later Georgian style, retaining its original window openings on the ground floor but sadly without their glazing bars. This building reflects the great wealth of the town in the brewing and malting period of the eighteenth and nineteenth centuries.

Reaching the junction with Kirkgate the building on our left was originally the Boar's Head Inn (see gable for the splendid original sign). This pub was a popular haunt of servicemen in both the First and Second World Wars.

Looking to the left along Kirkgate we see the Old King's Arms with its splendid coat of arms above the door. These are the arms of George IV (1762–1830) in whose reign it was

Above: The Prince Rupert – a
Wealden House.

Left: Decorative shop front in
Stodman Street.

called the King's Arms. Upon the accession of William IV this was changed to the Old King's Arms.

Turning around and looking up Kirkgate towards the church we see a splendid view of the church spire with some overhanging mediaeval buildings in the foreground.

Immediately on our right at the corner of Middlegate is one of those buildings. The timber-framed buildings of Newark were originally believed to date from the sixteenth century because this style of first-floor jetty was assumed to have taken fifty or more years to spread up the country from the South East. However, a major dendrochronology dating project some years ago, established that all of the Newark buildings dated back to some fifty or so years earlier than thought, putting them into the fifteenth century.

This building is particularly unusual in that it is jettied on two sides, which means that the first-floor corner is unsupported. This support is however achieved by means of a massive diagonal beam running across the building from the protruding corner. This beam often, as in this case, has a socket in the exposed end, which would carry a carved figure or grotesque. This may have led to such beams being called 'dragon beams' or it may just be a corruption of diagonal. The building also displays, at first-floor level, curved corner braces known as Kentish braces, another link with the southern wool trade.

A little further along on the left are two timber-framed houses of dissimilar construction. Looking across the street, the one on the left is of box-frame construction, a method requiring less large timbers, whereas the one on the right is of close studded construction, a more costly method requiring more timber.

These buildings belonged to the St Leonard's foundation, a body that traditionally cared for lepers in a building called the Spital outside the town walls. This building is locally known as Queen Henrietta Maria's house, as it was the house where Henrietta, Queen to Charles I, stayed when in town during the English Civil War. This building was probably considered a suitable residence for a queen because of its religious connections.

Again looking across the street we notice that there are a number of yards or doorways on the far side of the street. These are the remnants of the original planned medieval town of Bishop Alexander. Each burger or tradesman would have been allocated a plot, one rod or perch wide (approximately 5 m) that would run back as far as a back lane. The house would be built to end on the street and the rear of the plot would be used for growing produce and keeping livestock. When the town grew during the Georgian period these plots were serviced by an alleyway from the street and contained back-to-back houses and a privy in each yard. The alley was usually named after a public house or the owner of the yard.

Behind us as we look at the frontage across the road were the town's post office and associated buildings. Built in the reign of Edward VII by local builders, Brown and Co., it is a good, solid edifice as befitting its original purpose. The building is now cleaned and restored for its new life as the eponymous pub.

Past the archway to the original post office yard is the Gilstrap Hotel, the former home and business of Joseph, father of William Gilstrap the malster and benefactor.

Across the way is an ornate building of the late nineteenth century, originally built as the Smith's bank, later the Westminster bank and is now the home of the violin-making school. The building is by the Nottingham architect Watson Fothergill (he changed his

Above: The Old King's Arms in Kirkgate.

Left: View up Kirkgate.

Opposite: Timber-framed building on the corner of Middlegate.

name from Fothergill Watson). He was responsible for many fine buildings in his native city of Nottingham. The style is Venetian and it will be noticed that the windows at the two-story end are all different. It has been suggested that, because the building was a bank, which would be visited by wealthy clients, it could be used by the architect as his catalogue of design features.

We now reach the junction with Church Street and Wilson Street. Interestingly Church Street and Kirkgate mean the same but one in Saxon and one in Viking, indicative of the varied origins of the town.

Wilson Street, as we now see it, has only one side remaining. In the pre-Reform Act period of the late eighteenth and early nineteenth century, the voting franchise was linked to property ownership and in an open-voting system landlords could ensure that tenants voted for whom they supported. For this reason, Revd Bernard Wilson, vicar of the town, built this street in order to control the votes of the tenants. The street was originally two Palladian-style, brick terraces with end and centre pavilions. In order to improve the street and to open up the churchyard, the eastern side was demolished in the 1970s with the exception of the two end pavilions, and the remaining properties converted into flats.

7. Cartergate, Barnbygate and Appletongate

This stroll begins at Beaumond Cross. This part of the town was known as Beaumond in the Middle Ages, and a wayside cross, (now in Beaumond Gardens off London Road) was situated at the corner of the medieval town in this area.

The start of the stroll is by the red post box, a later box, at the site of the town's original first pillar-box. Walking along Cartergate, on our left we pass a shop with a double door up steps that was Newark's second Salvation Army Citadel, the original being in Millgate. A little further along we come to a timber-framed building of the fourteenth century, one of the oldest of such buildings in the town. Inside the entrance archway on your left can be seen a small section of stone wall which could be a remnant of the town wall.

Across the way a little further along is a pilaster, all that remains of the corner of the Warburton Temperance Hotel, formerly the home of Bishop Warburton.[1] Further along to the left is a doorway with a cast-iron pillar, all that remains of a door casing by the local foundry of Thomas Bradley.

Thomas Bradley took over the Wellington Iron Foundry on Northgate in Newark in 1874. In 1876, or sometime soon after, Thomas was joined in the business by his younger brother, William, the business being called T. & W. Bradley from then on. Thomas Bradley lived at Wellington House, Northgate, whilst William resided in Victoria Street.

In 1882 the Bradleys spent £1,000 on rebuilding etc. at the Wellington Foundry, taking the lease of the same for forty years at £80 per annum.

In the 21 February 1883 edition of the *Newark Advertiser* it was reported that the Bradleys had accepted the tender of Mr Crosland of Newark (£645 1s 6d) for erecting new warehouses and offices at the foundry. Subcontracts were taken by Messrs Dobney (joinery), Thrale (stone masonry), Bousfield (plumbing and glazing), Crossley (painting) and Dobbs (slating). The architect was R. W. G. Hayward of Newark who designed a wooden roof in one span to cover the 84-foot by 50-foot warehouse.

On 4 March 1885, the *Newark Advertiser* reported on the successful tender of Smith & Lunn (£72 12s) to erect a sixty-foot high chimney at the Wellington Foundry. The architect of the project being George Sheppard.

The business was merged in around 1921 with the Lincoln firm of engineers, Messrs Ruston & Hornsby Ltd. Thomas died six years later in 1927.

We next reach The Arcade, an Edwardian addition to the town providing a covered walkway lined with shops. This development was by Thomas Atter, a local shopkeeper and Mayor who owned the Old White Hart building and adjoining land.

Returning to Cartergate we see opposite two streets, Baldertongate, the original route of the Great North Road, and Barnbygate.

A short deviation into Barnbygate will bring us to the corner of Bede House Lane.

Site of Newark's first post box, Cartergate.

Stone walling in Cartergate.

Remnant of the Warburton Hotel.

Original picture of Warburton Hotel.

A Thomas Bradley cast-iron door pillar.

On our left is Barnbygate Methodist Church, built in 1846 as a Wesleyan chapel at a cost of £5,000; it is a fine example of a 'preaching house'. In the centre of the church is the pulpit, elevated so that those in the main part of the building and in the gallery can hear the preacher. Elevated further behind the pulpit are the choir stalls and an organ, all this enabling the traditional emphasis of preaching the word and praising the Lord to take precedent.

The church originally had box pews, now mostly removed to make the space more flexible. There is a pre-Raphaelite window in the northeast corner.

Across the road is a former Methodist New Connection church. This was a breakaway from the Wesleyans but in the last century a process of coming together by Act of Parliament of all the separated Wesleyan and Methodist churches resulted in the present Methodist Church being formed.

During the Second World War the building was used as a British Restaurant, a government plan to feed those families bombed out of their homes. These were closed in 1947.

The building through to Baldertongate then became the Kinema (later the Ritz) cinema. The old chapel is now apartments; the cinema on Baldertongate is a furniture store.

Next on the left is Bede House Lane, named after the Bede houses, almshouses of the Phyllypot charity. The original almshouses have gone but the small chapel remains, used for other purposes.

Almost opposite the entrance to Bede House Lane is the Devon (pronounced Deevon as the river) brewery (see plaque on the wall). Originally White's Brewery, it was acquired by John Goodwin who extended the premises through to Baldertongate and installed a new boiler. The water was drawn from an underground reservoir by three pumps. The brewery was taken over by Walter Shirley who renamed it Devon Brewery and continued to expand until it was merged with Warwick's and Richardson's in 1919.

We should return now to Cartergate and look through into the market by Bridge Street. This road to the market place was widened in 1832 to improve the entrance by removing the buildings on the left-hand side of the street.

Originally called Dry Bridge Street, it referred to the bridge over the mediaeval town ditch that ran across the middle of the street. This was in the vicinity of the line of tarmacadam, which interrupts the sets of the main surface about a third of the way along the roadway.

Cartergate now changes into Appletongate and we come to the east end of the church with its cross of sacrifice designed by Lutyens. The area was originally the church burial ground along with the land to the north side. Across the road on our right is a fine façade of brick houses; the house immediately opposite the southern church walk is an earlier vicarage and is a fine example of an early Georgian or Queen Anne house. It replaced the vicarage that stood on Parson's Mount to the north of the church.

Further along we come to the National Civil War Centre and Newark Museum. This building is the former Magnus Grammar School.[2] The bricks of the Georgian frontage were salvaged from the early vicarage mentioned above in 1817 by Reverend John Burdett Wittenoom, Master of the Grammar School. The Tudor hall dates from 1529.

Moving along again we come to the Palace Theatre. This area was formerly the site of the chantry, a house built to accommodate the several priests who serviced Newark's

many Chauntry bequests. On the dissolution of the chantries by Edward VI, the Crown sold off the land, and a fine Queen Anne house and deer park were established. The deer park is now the site of Newark (Lincoln) College.

In the early part of the twentieth century it came in to the possession of Mrs Emily Blagg who was the proprietor of her family engineering firm. Having no desire to live in the house, she demolished it and replaced it with a large theatre of eccentric design, which we see today.

Also on the right, past the theatre, was the county police station, now the college piano-tuning school. As mentioned, the County Police were a separate force to the Borough Police, whose station was in the town hall, until after the Second World War.

Opposite the police station/college are several yards, one of which has a barrel-shaped entrance for the passage of wide objects, such as barrels, to the houses behind. The second entrance, Jalland's Row, is a reminder of the yards as they were lived in, with back-to-back houses.

Moving further along past Magnus Street we come to the wall surrounding the Friary. This was a house of the Austin Friars or Augustinians. They provided the town with a social system, looking after the sick and providing alms for the destitute. Another more austere order also resided in the town, the Franciscan Observant Order. Both orders were closed by Henry VIII.

The buildings are now private apartments, and the grounds a public park that contains the remnants of a Civil War fortification, known as Lord Deincourt's Redoubt. This can be seen as a rise in the ground, near the Friary Road side of the Park.

We hope you have enjoyed our strolls around Newark, and we hope, too, that we have uncovered some of its lesser-known 'secrets'.

Opposite above: Plaque marking Devon Brewery on Barnbygate.

Opposite below: Barrel-shaped alleyway on Appletongate.

Notes

Entering Newark

1. William Jessop (1745–1814) Pioneer Civil Engineer
William Jessop is remembered as one of this country's foremost civil engineers, particularly famed for his work on canals, harbours and early railway lines.

He was chief engineer on the Grand Union Canal and the Erewash Canal on the Nottinghamshire/Derby border. He also worked on the Cromford Canal for Sir Richard Arkwright in Derbyshire. He was Chief Engineer for the Avon Docks at Bristol and the West India Docks in London.

Born in Devon in 1745, Jessop was taken on as a pupil by John Smeaton (the noted road builder) who also acted as his guardian following the death of Jessop's father, Josias. In 1790 William Jessop founded the Butterley Ironworks in Derbyshire with fellow engineer, Benjamin Outram.

Here they manufactured cast-iron edge rails for early railways, a design Jessop had used successfully with flanged wheels on a horse-drawn wagon way for coal in Loughborough.

He was also engineer on the Surrey Iron Railway of 1802.

In 1809 he designed the Floating Harbour at Bristol – an artificial lake formed by damming the tidal River Avon – without which the continued expansion of Bristol into a major port could not have occurred. It is still the largest enclosed stretch of water in the world.

The Newark connection – William Jessop lived in Newark from 1784 to 1805 in a house directly opposite the old police station on Appletongate (a plaque now commemorates his time there). He was a partner in the firm that ran Newark's cotton mill (Messrs Handley, Sketchley, Jessop & Youle), and was Mayor of Newark in 1790 and 1803.

It is sometimes erroneously stated that Jessop – living in the town as he did – was the engineer chosen to oversee the creation of the Newark Navigation below Newark Castle. This has now been disproven by Professor Stanley Chapman in his article 'The Newark Navigation: the development of trade and industry 1740–1880' in *Transactions of the Thoroton Society volume 117*.

2. Newark in the First English Civil War, 1642–1646
Newark's geographical position at the intersection of the Fosse Way and the Great North Road where it crossed the river Trent, gave the town enormous strategic importance. It was important for the King to keep this area under Royalist control, to keep open his lines of communication to his northern followers, and also to his route to Oxford where he had formed his new headquarters.

Relations with Parliament broke down and both sides attempted to raise armies. The King chose to raise his standard at Nottingham on 22 August 1642. A week later the standard was blown down in a gale and the King visited Newark to rally the citizens to his cause. He had visited previously, and seven regiments were raised from around Newark and were present at Nottingham.

Newark accepted his cause possibly because of his, and his supporters', land ownership in the town and area and also because of his frequent visits.

The Nottinghamshire-trained bands (the Territorial Army of the time) were mustered at Newark and Sir John Henderson was made the first military governor of the town in December 1642, after the Edgehill campaign and after Newark's townsfolk had beaten off an attempt by Parliamentarians from Lincoln to take the town.

Throughout the conflict there would be a military authority with the Mayor and twelve Aldermen as the civil authority. The Governor was based in the large timber-framed house in Stodman Street, near the corner of the Market Place. In all, there would be four governors – Sir John Henderson, from 1642 to 1643; Richard Byron (2nd Baron), October 1643 to 1644 (he replaced Henderson following defeats in Lincolnshire in October 1643); Sir Richard Willys, October 1644 to October 1645; John Belasyse (1st Baron), October 1645 to 8 May 1646.

The town's Aldermen sometimes held their meetings in the large schoolroom of the Magnus Grammar School, now the home of the National Civil War Centre.

On 23 October 1642, the battle of Edgehill in Warwickshire took place. The battle was narrowly won by the Royalists, but not decisively. It was a 'score draw' with both sides claiming victory.

In February 1643 the first Parliamentary forces were seen in the Newark area and the first siege began.

This first siege was short, just a couple of days, but with fierce fighting around Northgate near the Spital and around Beaumond Cross and Baldertongate. The Parliamentarians, led by Thomas Ballard, were finally driven off by a counter-attack led by Sir John Henderson.

This siege, whilst brief, was a foretaste for Newark of things to come. Siege warfare had become increasingly popular among the military as a means of warfare because of the unpredictability of pitched battles. There would be memories of the history of the Thirty Years' War, where the crown could change hands in a few hours of confused conflict.

Siege warfare was also being developed into a science on the continent. 'Sconce' was the Dutch word for 'fort' and had been developed by the Dutch, Swedes and Germans during the Thirty Years' War. It was a structure that could rapidly be constructed by soldiers. A sconce could stand up to bombardment by the large cannons of the day, better than a stone castle.

On 16 June 1643 Queen Henrietta Maria arrived in the town with a force of 4,500 men. She had been on the Continent, securing arms and mercenaries for the Royalist cause. Whilst at Newark she sent out a force under the commander of her army, Baron Dohna (a German mercenary), to attack Nottingham. The attack was repulsed and the commander killed; he is now buried in the churchyard with other Royalist officers. (They were originally interred in the church crypt, but were moved in the nineteenth century, and a bronze plaque commemorates them.)

On 29 February 1644, a force of 7,000 men under Sir John Meldrum surrounded the town, which they bombarded with cannons and grenades, day and night. This was the cause of damage to the church spire and a grenade destroyed the house of Alderman Hercules Clay. The cannons doing this damage were located on Beacon Hill between the town and the village of Coddington.

After three weeks of this treatment the town was becoming desperate. It is a measure of the value of Newark to the King that he sent his best commander, his nephew Prince Rupert of the Rhine, to relieve the town.

The Prince arrived in Bingham on the 20 March with 3,000 cavalry and 3,000 foot soldiers. He marched overnight to the top of Beacon Hill and early on the morning of 21 March, he led his horse in several charges down Beacon Hill and routed the Parliamentary forces, whilst the town's garrison, led by Sir Richard Byron, took 'The Island', causing the Parliamentarians to surrender their weapons before being allowed to depart.

In October 1645 the King made his last visit to the town. At this time his position was becoming perilous and Newark was his last stronghold in the North Midlands. In anticipation of the coming storm, the town was heavily fortified with an encircling rampart and ditch, together with two large sconces to command the approaches to the town. The King's Sconce, to the north, being raised by Byron during the second and third sieges, was levelled in the middle of the nineteenth century and is now under the Northgate Retail Park. However, the Queen's Sconce has survived intact and can be seen to the south of the town. It is the best-preserved Civil War earthwork in the country.

These arrangements were soon put to the test with the arrival of 7,000 Scottish troops and 9,000 English troops. The Scots occupied 'The Island', which was the area of land between Newark and Kelham, isolated by the western arm of the River Trent.

The English troops had their headquarters at Hawton (General Poyntz) on the southern and eastern side of the town. Despite this there were several sorties by the garrison causing a line of circumvallation to be constructed to contain the Royalist garrison and protect the besiegers.

Conditions in the town deteriorated badly as the months wore on. Food was short and infectious diseases were rife. Typhus raged in the winter and plague from March onwards. The lack of coinage caused the governor to stamp lozenge-shaped coins from salvaged (or plundered from Leicester) silver to supplement the King's coinage.

Although Newark held out, elsewhere things were collapsing for the Royalist cause. In May 1646 the King decided to try and negotiate with the Scots in the hope of persuading them to come over to his side. Only after it was clear negotiations were failing, was he forced to surrender.

In disguise he arrived at Southwell and on the 6 May, he attempted to negotiate with the Scots commissioners and once it was clear the negotiations weren't working, he was moved to the Scottish camp at Kelham House where he was kept the night before surrendering to General David Leslie, the Scots commander, at the Edinburgh Sconce. He wrote to the Governor of Newark, Lord John Belasyse, instructing him to surrender, from Rossiter's headquarters at Balderton. The Mayor of the town attempted to persuade the Governor to ignore the order and to 'Trust in God and Sally Forth' (now the town's motto);

however, the surrender terms were accepted and two days later the garrison was allowed to march from the town unhindered.

The Parliamentarians would appear to have left the town without looting, probably because of the fear of disease but instructed the townsfolk to destroy the castle and siege works. This work was carried out with little enthusiasm and accounts for the fact that we still have a large part of the castle and several siege works remaining. Subsequent 'looting' of the stonework accounts for much of its dilapidation.

The town was not involved in the second Civil War, which began whilst the King was being held at Carisbrooke Castle after he had tried to negotiate for the Scots to support him, in return for introducing Presbyterianism across his realm.

The town probably took many years to recover from the effects of the plague, which is why it missed the really early building boom and why it retains many of its timber-framed buildings today, especially those associated with the Civil War.

3. Lady Ossington and the Coffee Palace

In the Victorian era, there was a vociferous campaign against the 'demon drink'. Charles Dickens wrote works, such as The *Pickwick Papers*, which outlined the great damage brought about in the slums of the industrial cities by cheap, plentiful alcohol. In response, the Temperance Movement flourished, with organisations such as the Independent Order of Rechabites conducting propaganda campaigns against 'strong drink'. This was a worldwide movement, and in Australia a number of Temperance Hotels – known as Coffee Palaces – were established, to enable families to visit, knowing there would be no drunkenness, as well as furthering the aims of the movement.

Charlotte, Viscountess Ossington, the daughter of William Bentinck, the 4th Duke of Portland, and the widow of the 1st Viscount Ossington (who had been the Speaker of the House of Commons), was a very strong supporter of the Temperance Movement. So much so that in 1882 she caused a magnificent temperance hotel, complete with a bowling alley, bowling green, billiard room, tea garden and a stable block to be built, directly opposite the ruined Newark Castle, in the centre of Newark, Nottinghamshire. The building was to stand as a memorial to her late husband. She endowed it with the rents from various other properties in town. Her aim appears to have been to turn the local farming community, the tradesmen and the many commercial travellers who passed along the Great North Road, away from the consumption of alcohol. This seems rather whimsical, given that some of the major activities in and around the town included the production of barley and the brewing of beer.

Never the less, the Ossington Coffee Palace opened with great fanfare in 1882, and a plaque affixed to the building reads: OSSINGTON COFFEE PALACE. It is a perfect copy of a seventeenth century hostelry erected in 1882 as a temperance hotel by Viscountess Ossington, a daughter of the 4th Duke of Portland, and widow of first Viscount Ossington, one-time Speaker of the House of Commons. The building was built in brick and stone and fitted out with every 'modern convenience'. This did not help, however, as by 1891, the hotel was making a loss – this was perhaps not helped by the fact that the Board of Trustees paid themselves over £50, and the salary for the Secretary of the Board was the same.

During the First World War, the building was taken over by the War Department, as were many other large buildings. It staggered on into the interwar period, but was requisitioned in 1942 by the Air Ministry as accommodation for airmen. This is quite understandable, as the former RAF Winthorpe (now the site of the Newark Air Museum) is only 1.5 miles north-east of the town. Many members of the Polish Air Force (and other RAF personnel) trained at Winthorpe, and also undertook some operational sorties from there – there is a magnificent memorial cross to their fallen comrades in Newark Cemetery.

Despite being founded as a charity, it was established in the 1960s that the Coffee Palace had been operating as a commercial establishment, and therefore its position became untenable. The heirs of the Viscountess Ossington eventually sold the property, and the future of the building looked rather bleak for a while. Fortunately, a deal was brokered which allowed part of the building to be converted for residential use, and the rest occupied by a branch of the Zizzi Italian restaurant chain, who even boast that they have 'inherited' a benevolent ghost, which floats around the basement.

4. The Story of the Castle Gardens

Henry Ernest Milner was a landscape gardener and civil engineer active in the UK and abroad in the late nineteenth century. He was born in Liverpool, England on 18 April 1845, the son of landscape gardener Edward Milner (born 1819, died 1884). After an early career as a civil engineer, Milner joined his father's landscape-design practice in the 1870s.

Milner designed gardens in England, Scotland, Denmark and Sweden, and was author of *The Art and Practice of Landscape Gardening* published in 1890, which drew heavily on his father's designs. Milner died on 10 March 1906 at his home in Norwood, England and was buried in Darley.

Newark Castle Gardens were laid out in the 1880s as a Jubilee Memorial to Queen Victoria. The background to their acquisition by the town is set out in a booklet entitled 'Newark Castle Gardens' published in 1887 to promote the scheme. This states that, 'the approaching Jubilee of the Queen has naturally aroused a deep and wide interest amongst all her loyal subjects and it is earnestly felt that Newark ought not to be behind other towns in its determination to provide a lasting Memorial of so auspicious an event'.

The public was invited to contribute towards the project to convert the site of the Old Cattle Market round the foot of the Castle into 'public pleasure grounds for the free use of the people forever'. It was suggested that the gardens would be 'a constant source of health and pleasure, an attractive resort for the inhabitants' as well as giving Newark 'one of the finest entrances of which any town can boast', and adding largely 'to its residential attractions'.

The Cattle Market site had been given to the town earlier in the 1880s by William Gilstrap as part of his gift of a library, with the intention that the land would provide a stipend for a librarian. It was thought desirable however that the land become a garden and, to this end, the Viscountess Ossington offered £1,200 on condition that the site was 'laid out, planted, improved and maintained, for the purpose of being used by the public, free in perpetuity, as public walks and pleasure grounds'. This gift was bolstered by a sum of £500 from Alderman Henry Branston, leaving a sum of £2,500 to be raised by the town to complete the purchase of the desired area.

The Castle, and the Crown property embracing the ground lying between the ruins and Castle Gate, was acquired in 1889, and Henry Ernest Milner was called in to landscape the site. The Castle Gardens were opened on Queen Victoria's seventieth birthday, on 24 May of that year, and have remained a public park ever since.

Exterior of St Mary Magdalene Church

1. The Thomas Magnus Charity and his Schools

Thomas Magnus was born in Newark in about 1460, the son of John and his wife Alice who were innkeepers in the town. He was apparently a gifted child who was taken into the household of the Archbishop of York to be educated.

He then came back to Newark and was under the influence of Robert Brown, a wealthy Newarker who himself was the founder of a large Newark charity. It was Brown who recommended Thomas to a powerful churchman, Thomas Savage Archbishop of York.

By the turn of the century we find Magnus as an ordained priest acting as a trusted middle-ranking civil servant in the government of the north of England and entrusted with negotiations with Scotland.

He then shows up as a member of the household of Thomas Wolsey, the chief minister of Henry the VIII. In this capacity he travels to the 'Field of Cloth of Gold' in France with the royal party.

By the time of the falling-out between Wolsey and Henry, Magnus was an old man and was able to distance himself from the difficulties at court. In that period it was usual to reward clergy, acting as civil servants, with ecclesiastical livings. Magnus was no exception and acquired several, one at Collingham near Newark and his richest as Archdeacon of the West Riding of Yorkshire.

He retired to his living at Sessay in Yorkshire where he is buried, having lived to the great age of ninety.

Whilst there is no record of his education in Newark, his obvious affection for the town of his birth led him to leave his considerable wealth as a deed of gift of land, the rent income of which was to be used to provide Newark with a school for the teaching of song and a school for the teaching of grammar.

These two schools would provide free education for any boy of Newark and were administered by a trust made up of townsmen. The deed was very detailed and advanced for its time in that it gave the masters sick pay and two months' annual leave on the grounds that 'no one should be expected to stay in Newark for more than ten months of the year'. The master of the grammar school was not allowed to have other employment, a feature that was to cause friction with the master of the song school who was allowed to take in 'private' pupils.

There is very little record of the early school and over the years the gift has been altered to meet modern requirements, however the spirit of the original gift is still alive in the town. The gift allowed any surplus monies after payment of the masters' fees, to be used for the benefit of the town. As the town aldermen were also the trustees, it was in their interests to have as large a surplus as possible to spend in the town and therefore the wages of the masters were held down. The trust money was used for paving the town and for the provision of the original gas lighting. The song school still provides the church with a choir and choir/organ master and the trust is still able to support the Magnus Church of England Academy, which is the direct descendant of the original grammar school.

The school was in financial difficulties at the beginning of the twentieth century due in part to an agricultural recession lowering incomes and some bad management of the resources by the trustees. The school was saved and moved to its present site by the generosity of the chairman of the governors, Thomas Earp, who gave in excess of £10,000 to buy the site and build the present school.

The school has produced a number of nationally important people from its students. The earliest is Dr John Blow, organist at Westminster Abbey, composer and teacher of Henry Purcell. Few records exist of students until the twentieth century but several figures of the Victorian period are known to have been at the school. Gonville Bromhead, who won a VC at the battle of Rorke's Drift. Dean Hole the rose grower, Cartwright, anti-slavery campaigner, and Bishop Warburton.

These last four have the school houses named after them. The twentieth century has also produced its famous Magnusians. Donald Wolfit CBE the actor; Sir William Nicholson the artist; Sir Joseph Lockwood chairman of EMI; Godfrey Hounsfield CBE, FRS inventor of the medical scanner for which he was awarded a Nobel prize and Sam Derry, hero of the Rome escape line in the Second World War.

More recently, W. H. 'Dusty' Hare, England and British Lions full back, one time holder of the world points record in first-class rugby and John Wells, England A international, former head coach of Leicester Tigers.

Early in the nineteenth century, boarders were increased as they were not covered by the deed, which only covered boys from Newark, and they could be charged a fee. This practice continued until the 1944 education act when the school became an 11+ grammar school.

The grammar school continued until 1974 when all of Nottinghamshire became comprehensive. This was achieved in Newark by pairing the boys' and girls' grammar schools with the two secondary modern schools to produce a KS3 School (Magdalene High School) and a KS4/5 school (Magnus Upper School). In 1997 it was decided to merge the schools and so Magdalene High School with its Church of England Trust and Magnus Upper School with its Magnus Trust were merged to form Magnus Church of England School and eventually all education moved to the Earp avenue site.

Interior of St Mary Magdalene Church

1a. The Story of Hercules Clay

A worthy resident, Hercules Clay, sometime Mayor of Newark, resided in a house at the corner of the Market-Place not far from the Governor's mansion. For three nights in succession he dreamt that the besiegers had set his place on fire, and he became so impressed with the circumstance that he and his family quitted their abode. They had no sooner done so than a bomb, fired from Beacon Hill, occupied by the Parliamentary forces, and believed to have been aimed at the Governor's house, fell on the roof of Clay's dwelling, and, passing through every floor, set the whole building on fire. The tradition is that a spy, blindfolded, and bearing a flag of truce, came from the army on the hill to the Governor's house, and was able on his return so accurately to describe its situation as to make the shot all but successful. To commemorate his deliverance, Mr Clay left a sum of money to be distributed in charity (it is given away annually in penny loaves), and the memorial to him in the parish church testifies in a lengthy and curious inscription to the miraculous nature of his escape: 'Being thus delivered by a strength greater than that of Hercules, And having been drawn out of the deep Clay, I now inhabit the stars on high.'

It is an unusual tradition, although endowed sermons are not rare in England. Surviving ones are and certainly because of the association with the mayoralty and the colourful nature of its legend, its name Bombshell sermon kept it well known. A visitor reported:

I attended the ceremony on the warm Sunday 11th, the exact day of the incidence. The delightful parish church of Mary Magdalene rang out at 11.00 a.m. to call the assembled Mayor, local dignitaries and those in local business to the sermon. They processed with great solemnity from the Town Hall next door to Clay's residence and led by a bible bearer, said to carry Clay's bible or a replica. As we entered the church, two trays could be seen with bread buns wrapped in cling film, the penny loaves noted above. The vicar welcomed the assembled congregation, with the bible presented at the altar and the readings had a bread theme, the Sermon on the Mount, being the obvious one.

1b. Born and Bread
Whilst on the matter of food, it is worth considering these penny loaves, or now as it seems, buns. The provision of penny loaves was established from the profits of the £100 given by Clay. Penny 'doles' were often used to attract attendance to the sermon (as well perhaps a vestige of the old idea of sin-eating, lost at the Reformation) and gave the day in Newark another name, Penny Loaf Day. Reports in *The Mercury* for March 1828 record that 3,654 loaves were given out and it reports understandably with scorn: 'Some gentlemen amused themselves by kicking the bread around in the streets.' They noted that they believed that they would 'regret the waste if in the future they are hungry'.

Certainly the size of the dole and its misuse had an effect on how it was delivered, for in 1832, the parishioners met to discuss the fact the dole 'cost more than was left for that purpose' and deemed it necessary to restrict it to eighty poor and needy families by giving one-shilling loaves. However, this agreement did not appear to have had an impact, as in 1833 it is reported:

On Monday last, being the anniversary of the deliverance of Mr Clay from Oliver Cromwell's fury, a sermon was preached in the morning of Newark church and in the afternoon a penny loaf was distributed in the Town Hall to all who chose to accept it by the church warden according to the tenor of the will of Mr Clay three thousand eight hundred and sixty four loaves were delivered.

It appears at some point that the sermon died out, to be re-established in 1974, at first by the Newark Chamber of Commerce, but now by the Newark Town Council. The present ceremony invites local charities to do a presentation and it is to that chosen charity that the loaves are given. In 2012 it was Newark Foyer who provided for the homeless and they took the twenty loaves and, deciding to add bacon to them, gave them to anyone who came looking for help at the desks on the following Monday.

So I am sure that Hercules Clay would be happy to hear that the needy are once again receiving the dole.

Cartergate, Barnbygate and Appleton Gate

Please refer to note No 1 in section called The Thomas Magnus Charity and his Schools found in 'Exterior of St Mary Magdalene Church' notes.

Acknowledgements

The authors and publisher would like to thank the following people and organisations for the help given and use of material in this book: Parish Church of St Mary Magdalene, Newark (for permission to take photographs of the interior of the church); Glyn Hughes & Kevin Winter, Newark & Sherwood Museum Service, for the use of the photograph of John Smeaton, and advice on content, picturethepast.org.uk for permission to use the photograph of the Warburton Hotel in Cartergate; Patty Temple, Curator of Newark Town Hall Museum & Art Gallery, for permission to take photographs in the Town Hall interior; George Wilkinson, for many questions answered; Tim Warner, Development Officer, Local Studies, Nottinghamshire County Council, for permission to use contents of previous articles and for general support.

The authors took all other photographs.

Every attempt has been made to seek permission for copyright material used in this book. However, if we have inadvertently used copyright material without permission or acknowledgement we apologise and we will make the necessary correction at the first opportunity.